Into The Wild
Shadow Work Journal

RECLAIM YOUR WHOLENESS

By Dominica Applegate

Copyright © 2020

The information contained in this book is for general information purposes only and should not be considered a substitute for the advice of a mental health professional.

rediscoveringsacredness.com

for all who suffer

walk your own journey.
be unashamedly you.

TABLE OF CONTENTS

INTRODUCTION

I thought life would go differently than it has. Smoother, with fewer ripples. When I was a young adult, I thought I had it all together. I believed and portrayed to the world that I was the best friend, partner, Mom, Christian, etc.

I played the roles and wore the masks well, all while part of my personality - my shadow side - was growing quite large. I had no idea I'd become such a pro at stuffing parts of myself into my unconscious.

That is until a divorce in my mid-thirties popped that bag, unleashing a raging river of negative emotions that I had no idea how to cope with. My wounded inner child surfaced in a tantrum-like style, demanding to be seen, heard, and dealt with.

Thankfully, someone steered me toward the direction of shadow work, a time-tested tool that can help us face and integrate our shadow side. I put my work boots on and started digging into my psyche, shining the light of my consciousness onto those parts of myself that had been exiled to the dark.

We all have a shadow side. The parts of us that over the years we've repressed, hidden away, rejected, or ignored. Parts of us that we don't want anyone to see. Parts of us that **we** don't see.

There may be shadows that have been deemed negative, such as shame, trauma, painful memories, horrible thoughts, faulty belief patterns, fear, secrets, and more. There may also be shadows deemed positive, such as hidden talents, gifts, and traits.

If you desire to experience more emotional and spiritual wholeness, consistent shadow work will be an important part of your journey. Carl Jung, the infamous Swiss psychotherapist who is known for his scope of work on the unconscious, writes:

"Everyone carries a shadow, and the less it is embodied in the individual's conscious life, the blacker and denser it is."

The reality is that if we don't take time to journey within and explore, our shadow bag is likely to grow big and fester. The "long bag that we drag behind us," as poet Robert Bly describes it, doesn't just magically dissolve. It tends to grow in intensity and unconsciously wreak havoc in our lives until we consciously face, feel, and deal with what's been hidden.

Can you feel it? The weight upon your shoulders? Accumulated baggage? Unhealed pain?

The fact is that a dark shadow at max capacity won't serve us well. It can cause plenty of painful, disheartening, repetitive issues throughout life, such as repeat toxic relationships, chronic anxiety, addictive behaviors, and negative emotions like depression, rage, shame, frustration, and more.

The good news is that shadow work can be life-changing. When done consciously and consistently, you can transform the dense energy of the shadow side into psychological, emotional, and spiritual growth.

You can begin to fully own and embrace who you truly are - the light and the dark aspects of you - completely accepting your whole self.

What Is The Shadow?

According to Jung, the psyche is comprised of various parts, including consciousness, ego identity, and the shadow, or unconsciousness. There's more to the concept, but let's keep it simple.

Essentially, from the time you are born, your mind takes the experiences, memories, traumas, negative emotions, and so on that the ego does not know how to process, or they're just too shocking, and exiles them into the shadow. Things that society frowns upon goes into there as well.

This may include the anger we didn't want to feel, the shock from trauma, the pain of neglect or abandonment, and so on. It may also include positive parts of us that we've split off from over the years. Maybe your parents thought you should be seen and not heard, so you repressed your voice. Or perhaps you were told that artists never amount to anything, so you stuffed your desire to create art.

Regardless of how the shadows that hide in the psyche came to be, we don't have to let them subconsciously rule our lives.

The Shadow Side Is Not Bad or Evil

The shadow side is dark, but not because it's bad or evil. It's dark because it's yet to be illuminated by the light of your consciousness. You haven't gone within and flipped the light on just yet, or maybe you've only turned the dimmer lights on.

Shadow work is grabbing a flashlight and setting out on an inner journey to explore your unknown inner landscape. It's casting light on the shadows that have been tripping you up or causing you pain, not so you can beat yourself up.

Rather, you're going into the dark to ultimately, free yourself of an overabundance of pain and bring forth your beautiful light.

Because when we can illuminate, face, feel, and deal with shadows, we release the pent-up energy associated with them. We integrate that accumulated energy back into the whole psyche, and as a result, experience more things like peace, joy, unconditional love, confidence, creativity, clarity, contentment, and fun.

Shadow work is a transformational inner journey toward greater self-discovery, meeting and embracing every aspect of you. Here lies an opportunity to stop running, acknowledge the immense pain you feel, stop the self-loathing, let your walls fall, deal with what you've been hiding or self-medicating, and begin your inner healing journey. Compassionately own and embody your whole self, shadows and all.

If there's one thing I know, it's that we all desire to grow to become more peaceful, authentic, enlightened, compassionate, and loving. Shadow work is a valuable tool to help you fearlessly embrace your shadow side and awaken to your true, whole self.

Throughout history, there's been a lot of pressure put on humans to be and act a certain way. You may feel pressured to be perfect, achieve success at any cost, be ultra-strong, ultra-independent, ultra-wealthy, stiffen your upper lip, keep up with the Joneses, and so on.

It can feel quite overwhelming.

It is my desire that this journal may give you the opportunity to begin a path toward becoming curious about your inner world. To start deconstructing your ego-identity and see what's underneath all the layers. To become interested in what's been exiled to your shadow bag for the purpose of facing, feeling, dealing, and integrating it.

Jung says, "There's no coming to consciousness without pain." It's time to mine the shadow caves, seeking out what's wanting to be noticed and dealt with. With courage and intent, you'll be well on your way to coming to know and love yourself on a whole new level. As humans, we have the opportunity to grow and mature – not just physically – but emotionally and spiritually. We can go from living life mostly unconscious to enjoying life as pure, loving awareness.

But it takes some work, dear one. The kind of work that can help bring more wholeness to each one of us and the collective.

How Will I Feel Doing Shadow Work?

Shadow work evokes different feelings or intensity of emotions for everyone. However, common emotions you may encounter along your journey are:

Fear: If you're like most people, the thought of going inside to face your deepest, darkest side elicits fear. Depending on your past, the intensity of fear can vary greatly.

My son recently told me that he has recurring nightmares where this huge, black blob is coming to devour him. He says he experiences sheer terror. He wakes abruptly, quite flustered for a while.

It's not uncommon for the shadow side to try to get our attention in dream time through frightening images.

Jung wrote about this, saying, "The most terrifying thing is to accept oneself completely."

Anxiety: Diving into the past or owning shadows can provoke anxiety. Again, the intensity will vary. I used to feel like anxiety would literally kill me. It was that intense.

However, between integrating shadows and using some helpful anxiety-reduction breathing techniques, the anxiety has decreased greatly. If anxiety arises, take advantage of the many anxiety-reduction techniques available.

Shame: It's common to encounter feelings of shame or embarrassment. There may be plenty of shadows trying to keep you feeling disappointed and ashamed. Don't let them.

Shadow work can help you silence and integrate such shadows, and this can feel quite freeing. We are light and dark, conscious and unconscious, and it can feel freeing to acknowledge this.

Anger: Some journal prompts may cause anger to surface, perhaps even rage. Even those who don't consciously feel angry may have rageful parts, especially if you're used to being a good boy or good girl because that's all that was acceptable in your home.

Shadow work can help you identify repressed anger or rage and learn how to express it in healthy, creative ways.

Numbness: You may not feel much at all, known as emotional numbness. Or you may not remember much about your childhood. When I first started shadow work, I couldn't remember much about growing up, so my answers were short. If you find this happening to you, it's alright. You may circle back around later and perhaps be able to remember more. If not, that's alright too. You don't have to remember everything in order to heal or integrate shadows.

If you've lost touch with your emotional guidance system, or you've numbed out with addictive behavior, shadow work can help you begin to reconnect, remember, deal and feel what wants to be healed in your shadow side.

Other emotions that may arise are guilt, regret, sadness, frustration, feeling abandoned, grief, and more.

If you start to feel like it's too much or too overwhelming, take some time to breathe slowly and deeply. Sit quietly or meditate for a bit and come back to journaling later. Take it at your own pace. There's no rush.

As you work through the prompts, consciously give yourself compassion and doses of love. If it feels like too much, consider working through the questions with a professional.

Remember that as you work through the shadow work journal, you're getting in there deep and re-collecting parts of you that you've chipped off over the years. You're becoming more whole.

Practicing Mindfulness & Meditation

Diving into unknown inner territory can feel daunting. While it's great to illuminate your hidden talents and positive traits, discovering your deepest, darkest secrets, trauma, evil thoughts, twisted fantasies, mistakes, cruel behaviors, agonizing loneliness, and more can mess with the mind. Adopting the practices of mindfulness and meditation can help.

What Is Mindfulness?

To be mindful means to consciously be in the present, aware of thoughts and feelings arising in the now. To be mindful is like being a thought detective. You're on the lookout for thoughts and emotions that arise. When you spot them, you can do some investigating.

If the thoughts are negative or false, you get to say so. You get to call them out and say, "Excuse me. I see you, and I'm not falling for that. I choose to believe and live in the truth, and nothing you say can cause me to believe otherwise."

You also get to notice the positive thoughts or belief systems you've relegated to the shadow side.

"Oh, hey assertiveness. I see you. I'm sorry I banished you to the shadow. I welcome you back into my life, in balance, of course. I need you to help me deal with a boss that's totally taking advantage of my niceness."

To be more mindful means that you live more in the present, using your five senses to keep you grounded there. Throughout the day, take time to bask in the present. To see and hear what's around you, feeling the ground beneath your feet and noting any smells or tastes.

Being mindful can help you remember that you're not your mind. You're not the stories going on in the mind, the conditioning, the traits, memories, and so on.

When you're present with *what is* (in all of its glory) in the moment as your true self, you're able to fully enjoy the bliss of reality. You notice what arises, such as thoughts, emotions, identity, etc., but *you're not those things*.

You are loving awareness.

To learn more about mindfulness, check out the many excellent websites and articles online about the topic. You may even want to check into free mindfulness apps.

What Is Meditation?

Meditation is a technique that can ultimately help you experience more peace in your mind. In the same way you exercise your muscles to train for a competition, you can meditate to train your mind.

Meditation is taking time to get quiet with yourself. It's going within as a sacred act, allowing thoughts to come and go while remaining detached as a witness. Thoughts are bound to arise, but we have the choice of what types of thoughts we identify with and what types we ruminate on.

If you're not keen on meditating, that's alright. Perhaps you can calm your thought world with a different practice or technique. If you'd like to become a regular meditator, do a bit of research to see what meditative techniques appeal to you.

As you commit to a regular meditation practice, you can get more acquainted with the "I" that is your core, spiritual nature. Your essence. The "I" outside of shadow and ego. You can connect with a space of peace, harmony, and all that is sacred.

Make a commitment, even if it's just five or ten minutes a day. Meditation is a practice and can certainly help you as you navigate the shadow side of your ego.

Working Through Journal Prompts

Take your time working through the prompts. If you come across something too challenging, skip it. Maybe it's just not time to address that yet. If you have experienced childhood or adult trauma, neglect, abuse, have been diagnosed with a mental health disorder, or you're simply not sure you want to confront your shadow side on your own, there are professionals that can help.

A counselor, Jungian coach, shadow work coach, spiritual advisor, wise friend, sponsor, etc., can oftentimes hold the space for you to begin processing and heal various wounds.

Remember, you're not going into the shadow to pulverize what you find. As mentioned, the shadow side isn't considered "bad" or "wrong". It's a construct, but still, a part of you that wants to be seen, heard, and brought back into your wholeness.

Go easy on yourself. This isn't about right vs. wrong. Cut yourself some slack as you delve deep into your psyche.

You don't have to have it all figured out or have all the answers. Do the work, but also allow your inner healing to unfold organically. The psyche is a complex construct that oftentimes helps us integrate shadows naturally. In dream time, for example.

Finding and Loving the Real You - Pure Awareness

Your inner journey unearthing and integrating shadows not only helps you grow psychologically and emotionally, but also spiritually. You're getting in there to expose your "false self" or your "ego identity", so, you can awaken to the reality of your TRUE SELF or spirit. The you that you've forgotten about or lost over the years! That innocent, pure, lovable, compassionate, generous spirit.

My hope is that you experience deep and profound spiritual transformation, as well as compassion and divine Love for yourself and others as you discover and embrace your shadow side.

Remember, it's progress we're after, not perfection. Doing your inner healing work can be a sacred act. Give yourself permission to do it with grace and acceptance. Stay connected to your heart space as you move forward, focusing on your breath.

Shadow Work Tips:

You may get triggered by completing a question. A trigger is an intense feeling or reaction. Realize that this is an opportunity to begin facing, dealing, feeling, and healing. This means resisting the urge to project the uncomfortable emotions onto another. This means consciously working through them, feeling, and then releasing them, so they will lose their power or charge over you.

Keep in mind that shadow work is not a one-size-fits-all approach to emotional, mental, or spiritual freedom. And it's also not a "one and done" kind of thing.

Shadows are often layered. You may face, feel, heal, and integrate one layer, only to have a variant or deeper version of it show up somehow down the road.

It's not enough to just learn about shadow work at the intellectual level. You want to learn and be able to apply it to your life consistently.

The following are four basic tips that can help you integrate shadows as you discover them via triggers, through journaling, through your nightly dreams, and so on.

1: Acknowledge the Emotion That Arises

As a shadow hunter, from here on out, you're going to be on the lookout for what you're thinking and feeling at any given moment. You're going to notice when you feel emotionally triggered or charged. As soon as you realize you're triggered, pause, and acknowledge it.

Notice and feel the emotions momentarily. Recognize this is a trigger. The more intense the feelings, the bigger the shadow is that's asking for your attention.

The sensations may feel intense at first, but know that by "feeling" it, you're working on "healing" and integrating it.

2: Observe Shadows as a Witness

You may discover plenty of things relegated to your shadow side, and not all of them are going to feel good. However, remember that those emotions, thoughts, belief patterns, stories, traits, etc. are not arising to hurt you. They are part of your shadow side that the mind has been creating since the time you were born.

It helps to observe shadows as they arise from the perspective of your true self or spiritual nature. Refer to the thoughts or emotions that arise as "it," "you," "them," "exiled energy," etc.

For example, rather than saying, "I am depressed", you could say, "I see you, Depression. I feel you quite nicely right now." This way, you're not identifying solely as depression. "I am unworthy" can be rephrased as, "I feel you, Unworthiness."

You can begin to witness shadows from the space of loving awareness, recognizing that the shadow part of you isn't reality. It's a created construct, just like your ego. But it's not the real you as a spiritual being or consciousness.

3: Detain and Question

The next thing you can do is detain and question what's arising. Continue to act as a detective, doing some inner inquiry. You can ask things like, "Where did you come from?" "What do you want?" "Why do you keep popping up?" Feel free to journal the answers if you can at that moment.

4: Consciously Integrate

Once you've felt it, acknowledged it, observed it, and questioned it, now it's time to lovingly bring it back into your psyche, otherwise known as integration.

Remember, emotions are energy in motion. They have messages for you. That repressed, suppressed, rejected energy wants to be seen, heard, and lovingly processed and released. Rather than resist them, embrace them and let the sensations move through you, dissolving into what may feel like more wholeness. Enjoy the peace that comes along with it.

Repeat these four steps each time you're contending with intense emotions that arise. Resist the urge to project your feelings onto others when you're emotionally agitated.

Rather, do some inner inquiry before responding. It may only take a few moments, but it's worth it if it can help you heal and integrate shadows and save you from projecting your pain onto others.

This is a sacred time for you. You are shining the light of your consciousness into the darkness, not knowing what you'll find. That uncertainty can feel scary. But take heart, this inner exploration can lead you to really understanding that you are not, nor have you ever been, that baggage that you've been lugging around.

Let the digging begin, as you walk your path toward rediscovering your beautiful sacredness.

> "Who looks outside, dreams;
> who looks inside, awakes." Carl Jung

Remember, all the answers you need are inside of you; you only have to become quiet enough to hear them.

debbie ford

Caregiver Traits

Make a list of three negative and three positive characteristics of your primary caregivers who raised you. What is it you liked most about each caregiver? Do you have any of these positive or negative traits? Which ones? How do they manifest in your life? Do you recognize any patterns?

_____

_____

_____

_____

_____

_____

_____

_____

_____

_____

_____

_____

_____

_____

_____

_____

_____

_____

_____

_____

_____

_____

_____

i am so worthy

Fear of Darkness

Were you afraid of the dark as a child? Explain a situation when you were quite afraid and why. If you start feeling anxiety or fear as you write, distance yourself and observe the feelings. Dig around a bit to see if you can pinpoint the root cause. Is there a particular fear underlying the feelings? Abandoment? Rejection? Insecurity?

_____
_____
_____
_____
_____
_____
_____
_____
_____
_____
_____
_____
_____
_____
_____
_____
_____
_____
_____
_____
_____
_____

i believe in goodness

Memory Deletion

Is there a memory you have that you would like to delete forever? If so, what is it? How would deleting the memory of it impact your life today? How would you feel? Is there a second memory? Go ahead and share.

i choose to focus on love today

No Holding Back

Let your shadow side speak to you all the negative things you think it wants to say. Don't let it hold back. An example would be, "You are so lazy. And stupid. You'll never amount to anything."

Once you're done, confront that shadow side. Let it know that those negative words are just words and they can't hurt you anymore. Let it know that even if you are _____ at times, it's alright. You're also the opposite! (Lazy vs. Energetic, Shy vs. Assertive). Let it know you're growing more and more conscious of you as LIGHT, as GOODNESS, as PURITY, as WHOLE.

_____
_____
_____
_____
_____
_____
_____
_____
_____
_____
_____
_____
_____
_____
_____
_____
_____
_____
_____
_____
_____

i am good. pure. light.

Mirror Work

Look directly into your eyes in a mirror for a minute. Relax as you do so. What kinds of thoughts or feelings arise? Is it uncomfortable? Do you feel silly? More spiritual? Self-aware? Mirror work can be a powerful tool to see what's lurking in your shadow side, as well as remind you of your authentic, spiritually evolved self. Write about your experience.

_____

_____

_____

_____

_____

_____

_____

_____

_____

_____

_____

_____

_____

_____

_____

_____

_____

_____

_____

_____

_____

_____

_____

_____

i am waking up more every day

Draw Your Shadow Side

Draw a picture of your shadow side. How do you see it? What kinds of thoughts, beliefs, emotions, traits do you think are in it?

Positive & Negative?

_____

_____

_____

_____

_____

_____

_____

keep doing the work. it's worth it.

A Letter to Your Ego

Make a list of negative characteristics you identify with about YOU. (Anxiety, depression, rage, fear, poor work ethic, lack of discipline, commitment, etc.) Then, embody the spiritual part of you that doesn't see any of those characteristics or traits. Write a letter from this "already whole" part of you to that part that's struggling. Be gentle.

_____

_____

_____

_____

_____

_____

_____

_____

_____

_____

_____

_____

_____

_____

_____

_____

_____

_____

_____

_____

_____

_____

_____

_____

_____

_____

_____

learn to quiet the mind

Maturity

Would you describe your behavior as mature? Are there times or instances when you feel you act immaturely? Write about this. What would those closest to you say about your maturity level?

_____

_____

_____

_____

_____

_____

_____

_____

_____

_____

_____

_____

_____

_____

_____

_____

_____

_____

_____

_____

_____

_____

_____

i am growing on all levels

Support Level

Do you feel supported by the Universe? Your higher power? Others? Make a list of those you know 100% you can count on if you truly needed something. If you find yourself lacking a support system, think about if you felt supported by your parents when you were growing up.

Could feelings of being alone, abandoned, or unworthiness be lurking in your shadow? Can you picture what your life would look like with a fantastic support system? Write about what that would look like and make a plan to go after that kind of support.

_____

_____

_____

_____

_____

_____

_____

_____

_____

_____

_____

_____

_____

_____

_____

_____

_____

_____

_____

_____

_____

_____

all is well

Relationship Toxicity

Do you have any unhealthy relationships in your life right now? If so, with who? Have you addressed the unhealthy aspects of this relationship with them? Do you feel they are solely to blame? What is it that you don't like about these relationships? How do they make you feel? Can you see a pattern? {If so, it may help to explore in therapy.}

_____
_____
_____
_____
_____
_____
_____
_____
_____
_____
_____
_____
_____
_____
_____
_____
_____
_____
_____
_____
_____
_____
_____

i am ablaze with love

"When we find ourselves in a midlife depression, suddenly hate our spouse, our jobs, our lives, we can be sure that the unlived life is seeking our attention.

When we feel restless, bored, or empty despite an outer life filled with riches, the unlived life is asking for us to engage.

To not do this work will leave us depleted and despondent, with a nagging sense of ennui or failure. As you may have already discovered, doing or acquiring more does not quell your unease or dissatisfaction. Neither will "meditating on the light" or attempting to rise above the sufferings of earthly existence.

Only awareness of your shadow qualities can help you to find an appropriate place for your unredeemed darkness and thereby create a more satisfying experience. To not do this work is to remain trapped in the loneliness, anxiety, and dualistic limits of the ego instead of awakening to your higher calling."

Robert A Johnson

Admiration

What do you most admire in others? Why do you think that is? Do you see these traits anywhere in you? If not, do you want to acquire them? If so, how can you do that?

_____

_____

_____

_____

_____

_____

_____

_____

_____

_____

_____

_____

_____

_____

_____

_____

_____

_____

_____

"The most intense conflicts, if overcome, leave behind a sense of security and calm that is not easily disturbed" C. Jung

Energy Suckers

Describe a situation where you walk away feeling drained. Contemplate reasons this may occur. Then, write down some things you can do to address this situation. Can you avoid it? If not, can you address it by setting boundaries?

_____
_____
_____
_____
_____
_____
_____
_____
_____
_____
_____
_____
_____
_____
_____
_____
_____
_____
_____
_____
_____
_____
_____
_____

it feels so good to shed layers

Distractions

How have you been distracting yourself? In what ways? Overly busy? Workaholic? How long have you been distracting yourself? Why do you think you do this? Is it scary to be in the silence?

What can you do to stop this behavior? To slow down? Be still?

_____

_____

_____

_____

_____

_____

_____

_____

_____

_____

_____

_____

_____

_____

_____

_____

_____

_____

_____

_____

_____

_____

_____

_____

i am staying on task. yay for me!

Addictions

Are there any addictions present in your life? What are they? When did they begin? What are you getting out of remaining addicted to these things? Were either of your parents stuck in addiction?

If you have an addiction, are you willing address it? How? Make a plan.

_____
_____
_____
_____
_____
_____
_____
_____
_____
_____
_____
_____
_____
_____
_____
_____
_____
_____
_____
_____
_____

i am aligned with love

Persistent Negative Thoughts

What are the most common negative thoughts you think or speak about yourself?

Any idea where you picked up these types of thoughts/beliefs? What can you do to entertain more positive thoughts?

_____
_____
_____
_____
_____
_____
_____
_____
_____
_____
_____
_____
_____
_____
_____
_____
_____
_____
_____
_____
_____
_____

shadow work is courageous

Judgments Against You

Do you feel like others judge you? If so, how? Do you feel like those judgments are true indications of who or how you are? How do you react when you're judged? How often do you judge?

_____
_____
_____
_____
_____
_____
_____
_____
_____
_____
_____
_____
_____
_____
_____
_____
_____
_____
_____
_____
_____
_____

A man who is unconscious of himself acts in a blind, instinctive way and is in addition fooled by all the illusions that arise when he sees everything that he is not conscious of in himself coming to meet him from outside as projections upon his neighbour. Carl Jung

Insecurity

In what ways do you feel insecure? Are you more insecure with particular people? If so, who? Have you always felt insecure?

Are you familiar with what Attachment Style you are? (Secure/Insecure) If you're not sure, take time today to research to discover your style. It may help you to know as you continue learning about yourself.

_____
_____
_____
_____
_____
_____
_____
_____
_____
_____
_____
_____
_____
_____
_____
_____
_____
_____
_____
_____
_____

i am becoming more confident

Top Fears

What are your top three fears in life? Share a story surrounding them. Relax as you write. Remind yourself that you are alright right now. Breathe slowly. Notice any body sensations that occur as you write. (tenseness, tingling, heat, etc.) Breathe through them, with continued focus on relaxing. If you become overwhelmed, stop. Focus on something that makes you feel happy.

i choose faith over fear

Over-reaction

Do you tend to overreact? Describe a situation where you did so, then try to track the underlying thoughts, beliefs, or emotions causing the overreaction. Are you dealing with chronic stress? Childhood wounds that haven't been healed? It may be helpful to start learning what "triggers" intense reactions. Then, you can begin healing those shadow parts.

i trust myself and my higher power

Safety Level

Do you feel that the world is a safe place? Do you feel safe? Where is it that you feel the safest? Why do you think that is?

How can you create more feelings of safety in your life? Internally and externally.

_____

_____

_____

_____

_____

_____

_____

_____

_____

_____

_____

_____

_____

_____

_____

_____

_____

_____

_____

_____

_____

i am safe. i enjoy feeling safe.

"One does not become enlightened by imagining figures of light, but by making the darkness conscious. The latter procedure, however, is disagreeable and therefore not popular." Carl Jung

Belittled

Have you been belittled? Demeaned? If so, how did that make you feel? Share one experience when this happened. How did you handle it? Are you repeatedly being belittled? If so, are you willing to learn more about setting and keeping boundaries?

i am assertive when necessary

Conflict Resolution

When you find yourself in conflict with someone, do you fight, flight, freeze, or fawn (people please)? Are you good at conflict resolution? Or are you a runner? Do you "ghost" people? Do you scream? Shut down? Explore the topic. How did your parents handle conflict?

_____

_____

_____

_____

_____

_____

_____

_____

_____

_____

_____

_____

_____

_____

_____

_____

_____

_____

_____

_____

_____

_____

_____

_____

i am committed

Habits

Do you have a habit that could be causing negative issues or emotions in your life? Talk about that habit. When did you first pick it up? How do you feel about learning how to stop that negative habit? Do you believe you can?

_____
_____
_____
_____
_____
_____
_____
_____
_____
_____
_____
_____
_____
_____
_____
_____
_____
_____
_____
_____

i am becoming whole

What's Your Enneagram Type?

What Enneagram type are you strongest in? Now, look at the unhealthy characteristics of that type and list what ones are active in your life currently. How are they showing up? Which ones have you overcome? Look at the healthiest level of your type. What traits are showing up?

How does it feel to know you can aspire to reach the highest level of traits? Shadow work is helping get you there.

_____
_____
_____
_____
_____
_____
_____
_____
_____
_____
_____
_____
_____
_____
_____
_____
_____
_____
_____
_____
_____
_____

i am living authentically

Assessing Judgments

Take a few days to be mindful of any judgments you make about others. In what ways do you judge them? Do you find yourself giving them advice? If so, is this advice more for your benefit or theirs? Now, think about if what you are judging them for is present in you. Dig deep. At times, pointing fingers at others and judging them is actually judging a shadow part of ourselves that we've repressed, rejected, or hidden away.

i am healing

Worldview

Do you feel you are more concerned about yourself, others, or the world? One model of increasing consciousness discusses four stages:

Egocentric (I am most important)
Ethnocentric (My family/religion/tribe is most important)
Worldcentric (All humans matter regardless of race, religion, sexuality...)
Kosmocentric (All humans, the planet, the cosmos I value and support the same.)

Where do you think you fit in the stages? Why do you think that?

_____
_____
_____
_____
_____
_____
_____
_____
_____
_____
_____
_____
_____
_____
_____
_____
_____
_____
_____

i am generous

Playing Big or Small

Do you think you play small or big?

Do you minimize yourself or your potential? In what ways do you do each? When you play small, where do you think that originated? Did any of your parents play small? Where can you start playing "big" in terms of knowing your truth and purpose? Of acting on it?

_____

_____

_____

_____

_____

_____

_____

_____

_____

_____

_____

_____

_____

_____

_____

_____

_____

_____

_____

_____

_____

_____

_____

i am co-creating a good life

Feeling Hurt

Who is someone who has hurt you tremendously? Name the emotions you felt. Sit with those feelings for a few moments, noticing what sensations you feel in your body. Breathe through them.

Can you remember a time when you were young and felt that same feeling? If so, describe that situation. What would you'd like to say to that person? Remember as you write that you are NOT your emotions. Do your best to witness as an observer, feel the sensations in your body as you relax. Feel the intensity decrease as you observe.

_____
_____
_____
_____
_____
_____
_____
_____
_____
_____
_____
_____
_____
_____
_____
_____
_____
_____
_____
_____

i am here to learn & heal

Love Without Conditions

Can you love others without conditions? Without judging them?

Do you think people feel safe enough to be themselves around you?

Can you let them be them in the midst of their "stuff", even if it makes you feel uncomfortable?

_____

_____

_____

_____

_____

_____

_____

_____

_____

_____

_____

_____

_____

_____

_____

_____

_____

_____

_____

_____

_____

_____

i am non-judgmental

Ho'oponopo Practice

The Ho'oponopo is a Hawaiian practice of self-forgiveness that can help you clear out negative thoughts toward yourself. There are four simple steps.

Center yourself and say, "I'm sorry. Please forgive me. Thank you. I love you." Go ahead and expand on this some in writing. Think about a way in which you judge yourself, sabotage, or neglect yourself. Write about it. Then, write out the Ho'oponopo prayer concerning those areas.

i can and i am

Emotion Observation

Do you feel like an observer of your feelings? Or do you feel like you ARE your feelings? {I feel sad vs. I am sadness} {I feel angry vs. I am anger} {I feel shame vs. I am shame}

It is helpful to learn that we are not our emotions. We feel them, but as conscious spirits, we are NOT them. Write about how it would feel to be able to observe your feelings rather than fully feel them.

_____
_____
_____
_____
_____
_____
_____
_____
_____
_____
_____
_____
_____
_____
_____
_____
_____
_____
_____

i am determined

Suppressed Emotions

What emotions do you think you suppress regularly? Anger? Shame? Fear? Sit for a few moments and try to recall a time when you were young that you repressed emotions. Write down the situation, connecting with that emotion in your body. Practice feeling it, processing it, and breathe it out, letting it go.

_____

_____

_____

_____

_____

_____

_____

_____

_____

_____

_____

_____

_____

_____

_____

_____

_____

_____

_____

_____

_____

_____

i am letting go

Complaining

Make a list of your major complaints about others. Then, ask yourself what it is inside you that gets triggered by their words/actions. Fear? Worthiness? Lack of boundary setting skills? Trouble communicating? Pride? Envy?

By looking at what triggers us about others, we can learn a lot about what's lurking in our own shadow-side, bringing conscious light there in order to continue healing and growing.

_____

_____

_____

_____

_____

_____

_____

_____

_____

_____

_____

_____

_____

_____

_____

_____

_____

_____

_____

_____

_____

_____

i honor myself

Envy Exercise

Do you envy others? What they have? If so, what is it that they have that you desire?

How would it feel if you had those things right now? Do you think you can conjure up those feelings now? Go ahead and try.

---

i am content with what i do and don't have

Values

What do you value? What is important to you? How do you feel when someone doesn't value what you do? Share an experience where this occurred? {Examples: someone lied to you, someone with poor work ethic, someone who is mean to others, etc.}

Knowing what you value can help you experience those things that are important to you, increasing feelings of peace and joy.

_____

_____

_____

_____

_____

_____

_____

_____

_____

_____

_____

_____

_____

_____

_____

_____

_____

_____

_____

_____

_____

_____

i have values

Priorities

How often do you make yourself a priority? Do you think you practice self-care above all else? Do you find yourself complaining that you have nothing left to give often? That your cup is empty? If so, what does this mean regarding your priority of self-care? How can you improve this?

_____
_____
_____
_____
_____
_____
_____
_____
_____
_____
_____
_____
_____
_____
_____
_____
_____
_____
_____
_____
_____
_____

i embrace inner transformation

Inner Child Love

Find a picture of yourself as a baby or child. Consider framing it and putting it on your nightstand or somewhere in your home where you'll see it often. Use this picture as a symbol of your inner child who wants and needs you to parent him/her. Let it remind you that you truly are that precious baby/toddler/child and affirm your love for them daily.

breathe. slowly. deeply.

Shadow Monster

Close your eyes and picture your shadow side person in a dark cave. They're huddled in the corner in fear, not wanting your lantern to shine on them. They're dirty, and there are spiders and snakes all over the place. As you move closer, you notice how afraid your shadow side looks. Petrified. They don't want to be seen for the mess that they think they are.

Approach your shadow side with gentleness, compassion, and love. Let the light of your lantern reveal the truth – that your shadow side is clean, that the cave is but an illusion and you're both surrounded by white light. Sit beside your shadow side and put your arm around them. Comfort them. Let them know they are loved so much! That you'll never abandon them again. That it's safe for them to come out and get to know you. Enjoy life with you!

Write about the experience. How do you feel? How does your shadow side feel? How can this be a turning point for your life?

_____

_____

_____

_____

_____

_____

_____

_____

_____

_____

_____

_____

_____

_____

More writing space on next page

my light is always shining

i let the light in

Action

Is there something you know you should be doing but aren't? What is it? Make an action list of what you need to do to get it done, or at least start the process. Then, write how it feels to have done this task.

What could change in your life if you accomplish it?

_____

_____

_____

_____

_____

_____

_____

_____

_____

_____

_____

_____

_____

_____

_____

_____

_____

_____

_____

_____

_____

_____

_____

_____

i understand the value of step by step

Heroes

Who are your heroes? Why do you think you value them so much? Do you see those traits in you? Why or why not?

Were they there at one time and you've lost them along life's journey?

_____
_____
_____
_____
_____
_____
_____
_____
_____
_____
_____
_____
_____
_____
_____
_____
_____
_____
_____
_____
_____
_____
_____

i am my own super-hero

The Masks We Wear

In what ways are you wearing a mask? Acting inauthentic? Draw a picture of your masks and label them. (fake, secure, liar, etc.) How are they serving you? Do you have to continue wearing them?

Scribble them out one by one, acknowledging that it's alright to authentically be you.

_____

_____

_____

_____

_____

_____

_____

_____

_____

_____

_____

_____

_____

_____

_____

_____

_____

_____

_____

_____

_____

_____

i am not my masks

Broken Promises

Have you broken a promise to yourself?   Describe the situation surrounding this. (Let others cross boundaries, self-sabotage, etc.)

Take time today to forgive yourself. What would this feel like?

_____

_____

_____

_____

_____

_____

_____

_____

_____

_____

_____

_____

_____

_____

_____

_____

_____

_____

_____

_____

_____

_____

_____

_____

_____

i am doing great at being uniquely me

Negative Words

Look at the following words. Circle the ones that you identify with. Then, either go to a mirror or envision yourself in front of a mirror and own those words. For example, if you circled "afraid", say, "I am afraid!" If you circled "selfish", say, "I am selfish!"

Repeat it over and over with conviction until you can say it and you don't have a strong reaction. The point of this exercise is that you can identify with a shadow part with the purpose of stripping it of its power over you. Remember that on the opposite side of each negative word, there's a positive. (Fear/Faith, Selfishness/Generosity) When you can integrate the repressed part, you'll experience more of the positive aspects!

aggressive aloof boring bossy clinging compulsive cruel deceitful dishonest greedy impatient inconsiderate irresponsible jealous lazy moody narrow-minded overemotional rude selfish stubborn timid unreliable untrustworthy vain vengeful

More writing space on next page

i am brave

i am alright

Competition

How do you feel about competition? Do you think it's healthy? Necessary?

Have you always felt this way?

Were you like this as a child? With your siblings? Friends?

_____

_____

_____

_____

_____

_____

_____

_____

_____

_____

_____

_____

_____

_____

_____

_____

_____

_____

_____

_____

_____

_____

i am going easy on myself

A Letter to Self

Think about a time in your life that was quite challenging for you, where you aren't so proud of how you were in those moments. (Poor choices, addiction, mean, etc.) Take the time to write a compassionate and loving letter to that shadow part of you.

Be gentle, loving, and forgiving. Save the letter for times when you may need to encourage yourself.

_____

_____

_____

_____

_____

_____

_____

_____

_____

_____

_____

_____

_____

_____

_____

_____

_____

_____

_____

_____

_____

i am evolving

Diamonds in the Rough

Our shadow side may seem dark to us, but there are jewels to be found when we start digging around. Not all hidden aspects of our selves are "negative". We may have repressed positive aspects too, such as artistic talent, sensitivity, confidence, etc. Parts that we repressed or split from as children may indeed be like diamonds in the rough. Keep doing the inner healing work. Bit by bit, in doing so, you're integrating, coming together as a radiant, peaceful WHOLE person.

Write some affirmations down about yourself in various areas of your life. Write in present tense, such as, "I am peaceful throughout the day, trusting that God/Universe/Source has my back." Feel them as you write!

i love and approve of myself

Victimhood

Things can happen to prompt us to feel like victims. However, identifying with a victim mentality will likely keep you stuck feeling sad and powerless. Do you feel like a victim? That life is against you? If so, why? What happened?

Now, imagine you can fly. You can just think about rising up above the ground and it happens. Imagine you can rise above all those things that happened to you in life that caused you to feel powerless. You can soar above them and go on about your life experiencing more peace, joy, and love.

You can rise above a victim mentality. It will require you to take full responsibility for your life today and each day after, including your emotions. Painful things may have occurred, but today, you are not powerless. You can be powerful in thoughts, beliefs, and actions.

_____
_____
_____
_____
_____
_____
_____
_____
_____
_____
_____
_____
_____
_____
_____
_____

i am responsible

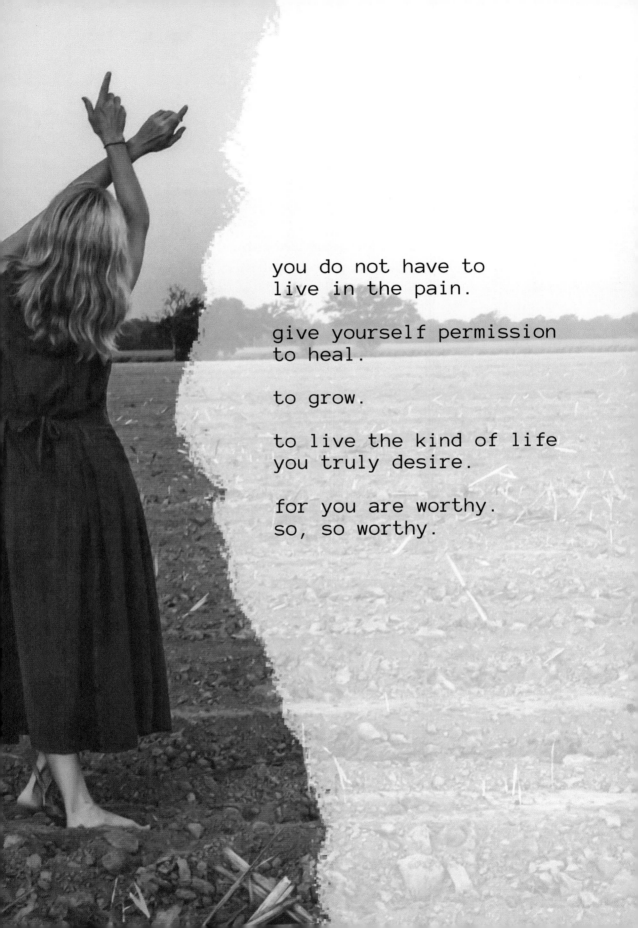

you do not have to
live in the pain.

give yourself permission
to heal.

to grow.

to live the kind of life
you truly desire.

for you are worthy.
so, so worthy.

Anger Levels

What makes you really angry? Who are you around when you feel this anger? Write about the last time you felt really angry. What happened? Who was there? What kinds of thoughts were running through your mind?

Then, become curious. Ask yourself why you feel so triggered? What is it in that person that angers you? Do you think you can stop pointing your finger at them and instead look within? See what IN YOU is being triggered? Is it fear? Shame? Victimhood? Lack of boundaries?

_____
_____
_____
_____
_____
_____
_____
_____
_____
_____
_____
_____
_____
_____
_____
_____
_____
_____
_____

i am safe

Unmet Needs

Does anyone in your life ever call you childish? Do you feel like a child sometimes? Act in childish ways? If so, write about some unmet needs your behavior may be trying to get that you didn't get when you were a child.

For example, if you find yourself whining regularly, what childhood need went unmet? Were your caregivers attentive to your needs? Your wants? How can you go about getting unmet needs today without resorting to childish ways? (Asking for what you want or need, aligning with your truth, being honest with yourself and others, etc.)

_____
_____
_____
_____
_____
_____
_____
_____
_____
_____
_____
_____
_____
_____
_____
_____
_____
_____
_____
_____

i have everything i need

Life as a Roller Coaster

Do you believe you should feel happy or peaceful all the time? Or are you alright with experiencing a roller coaster ride of emotions? We may have been taught as children that negative emotions weren't kosher, so we repressed them. We split from aspects of our SELF that threatened getting love from caregivers and society.

But now, as adults, we come to understand that it's alright to have negative emotions at times. Emotions are a guide and can teach us many things. Learn to become an observer of them. Sit with them. Let the speak to you.

Write a letter to yourself to prepare for a roller coaster ride. What would you say as you prepare for the incline? The decline? The loops? The emotions you might feel? How can you correlate this with life's ups and downs?

i'm grateful for the entire ride

Underlying Stories

Think about your primary caregivers. Can you think of an underlying story that might have been running their lives? Hidden beliefs? These can be positive or negative.

Just start writing what comes to mind about Mom or Dad. For example, if Dad was addicted to alcohol, what kind of story do you think was running in his mind? *I can't do this. Life is hard. It's too hard to face these feelings. Life sucks. I suck. I'm a failure. I'm scared. Nothing ever goes my way. I'm worthless. Etc.*

If Dad was happy and successful, it might be totally different. *I'm worthy. I'm diligent. I believe life is for me. I work hard. Things go my way. Etc.*

Take some time writing about Mom and Dad. Then, go through and see if you resonate with some of the underlying thoughts or stories. What are they? Look for the negatives and know that those are some of the shadows that may have been passed onto you. Acknowledge them and keep doing your own inner healing work to integrate them. You can also acknowledge the positive!

_____

_____

_____

_____

_____

_____

_____

_____

_____

_____

_____

_____

More writing space on next page

today, i will smile more

_____

_____

_____

_____

_____

_____

_____

_____

_____

_____

_____

_____

_____

_____

_____

_____

_____

_____

_____

_____

_____

_____

_____

_____

_____

i believe in myself

The Attraction Factor

If you've had romantic partners or have one now, what are some of the qualities that you found attractive about them? (If you haven't had a partner, what about a friend?) Make a list. Do you see a theme? What qualities do they have that you wish you had?

It's common to be attracted to those who express qualities that we'd like to express. (Confidence, communication skills, assertiveness, peace, optimism, etc.) Think about these traits and ponder whether you secretly want to have and express them. Do you think you can? Can you think of a time when you were young that you might have repressed this part of you?

i fully accept myself

The Past

Do you talk about your past a lot? Do others tell you this? Do you think more about the past than you do the present or future? It's common to get stuck in the past, using a lot of mental or emotional energy there. While it's alright to think about and talk about the past sometimes, it's helpful to learn to live more in the present and optimistically think about your future.

What do you want your future to look like? Write about your goals and dreams. Short and long-term. Smile and feel the excitement of co-creating this wonderful future with all aspects of yourself. You might even want to take this list or story and put it in a place you see often to remind you of your ideal future. See it, feel it, and know that you're indeed helping manifest it.

_____

_____

_____

_____

_____

_____

_____

_____

_____

_____

_____

_____

_____

_____

_____

_____

_____

_____

_____

my future is bright!

Control

Do you think you have to have control to feel safe? Have you ever been labeled a control freak? How does control show up in your life? What would it feel like to give up control?

Write about your observations.

i am a beautiful spirit

Light Shadows

Not every shadow is dark. In fact, we have plenty of "light" shadows, positive parts of ourselves that we may have repressed over the years. Make a list of some people (famous or not) that you truly admire. Then, write about the qualities you admire in them. Are they confident, compassionate, funny, etc?

It's quite possible that you've projected some of your light shadows onto them. You may indeed possess those very traits, but perhaps you've suppressed them. Take some time to think about this and own the traits you truly want to enjoy. Don't let fear stop you. Let those positive aspects of you SHINE!

i am shining brightly

Trigger Poem

What seems to trigger you more than anything at the moment? Write a poem about that trigger.

Write it in a positive light, even humorous.

Notice how you feel writing about that particular trigger.

_____
_____
_____
_____
_____
_____
_____
_____
_____
_____
_____
_____
_____
_____
_____
_____
_____
_____

*i am triggered less and less the more
i do my inner healing work*

Recurring Issues

What keeps popping up when you get into an argument with your partner/friend/parents? Is there a recurring issue? Do you find yourself pointing your finger with the same accusations/qualms? Take some time to write about your latest conflicts. What could be some underlying issues? Are you willing to truthfully look within to see if it's a part of your shadow at work?

Can you own it?

_____
_____
_____
_____
_____
_____
_____
_____
_____
_____
_____
_____
_____
_____
_____
_____
_____
_____
_____
_____
_____

relationships are opportunity for growth

Warrior of the Psyche

You are a warrior of your psyche, doing the inner work that needs done to integrate shadows and own your wholeness. Your inherent goodness, pureness. How does this make you feel?

How do you feel now that you've almost completed this Into The Wild Shadow Journal?

---

i am so loved

Surrender the Baggage

Picture yourself ten or twenty years older looking back at yourself now surrendering your baggage. By baggage, I mean those things you don't want to carry any longer. The shadows that have been weighing you down, like fear, shame, anger, disappointment, guilt, etc.

Write a letter from your future self to your self now. Write it with the knowledge that you surrendered that baggage and chose to live a mindful life dedicated to self-love, God-consciousness love, and other-love. A life free from those negative aspects.

What would your future "you" say? How would he/she encourage you?

_____

_____

_____

_____

_____

_____

_____

_____

_____

_____

_____

_____

_____

_____

_____

_____

_____

_____

_____

_____

goodbye baggage

Creative Vision

Write a short story in the present tense of the kind of life you truly desire. What's happening? How are you feeling? Be as specific as possible.

For example, *"Life is so amazing right now. I feel freer and more at peace than I've ever felt before. I wake up so grateful. My career is soaring and I'm loving the work. I'm also enjoying my new hobbies! My partner/spouse is incredible. We are connected at the heart level and growing individually and together. It's not perfect, but that's alright.*

When bumps come along in life, I'm not drowning in fight or flight mode. I'm living mindful, in expectation of goodness, and committed to showing up as my authentic self. Life is a roller coaster and I'm learning so much along the ride!"

_____
_____
_____
_____
_____
_____
_____
_____
_____
_____
_____
_____
_____
_____
_____
_____
_____
_____

things are always working out for me

Congratulations!

Robert A Johnson wrote, "To own one's own shadow is to reach a holy place - an inner center - not attainable in any other way."

Your story is important, all of it. As you worked through the prompts, I hope you were able to come to know your **whole** self much better.

I hope you have been able to own and integrate parts of your shadow that have been tripping you up in some way. And, that you've gained a lot of insight and discovered a lot of treasures.

Be proud of yourself for showing up and doing the work.

There are likely to be more layers, triggers that show up out of nowhere, and some surprises as you navigate life's road. Life tends to offer plenty of props or mirrors so that we can continually be learning, healing, growing, and evolving.

But it can all lead to greater experiences of peace and joy, and a greater knowing of who you truly are as spirit or pure awareness.

If you find yourself struggling now or in the future, consider reaching out to a professional therapist. It's worth the investment.

Stay present. Mindful. Breathe. Stay true to you.

Offer gratitude for it all.

dominica

About the Author

Dominica Applegate is a gentle soul showing up in this world to help others heal, grow, and evolve. She's especially interested in using her experiences and her story to encourage others to dive deep into inner inquiry to discover who they truly are.

For over ten years, she's reached many people globally with her inspirational writings about waking up, doing inner healing work, creating healthier relationships and enjoying a more meaningful life.

Professionally, she's equipped with a graduate degree in counseling and over ten years' experience working in the mental health field. Personally, she's been a serious seeker since her late teens, immersing herself in various spiritual practices.

Her books include:

- Healing After a Breakup: A 50-Day Devotional & Guided INNER WORK Journal

- Goodbye Codependency: A 40-Day Devotional & Guided Journal to Boost Self-Care

- The Pain, It Shapes Her World {Poetry}

Learn more at rediscoveringsacredness.com

Printed in Great Britain
by Amazon